D0805568

# Pet Rabbits
## UP CLOSE

by Jeni Wittrock

Gail Saunders-Smith, PhD, Consulting Editor

CAPSTONE PRESS
a capstone imprint

SHOREWOOD-TROY LIBRARY
650 DEERWOOD DRIVE
SHOREWOOD, IL 60404

Pebble Plus is published by Capstone Press,
1710 Roe Crest Drive, North Mankato, Minnesota 56003
www.capstonepub.com

Copyright © 2015 by Capstone Press, a Capstone imprint. All rights reserved. No part of this publication may be reproduced in whole or in part, or stored in a retrieval system, or transmitted in any form or by any means, electronic, mechanical, photocopying, recording, or otherwise, without written permission of the publisher.

**Library of Congress Cataloging-in-Publication Data**
Wittrock, Jeni, author.
Pet Rabbits Up Close / by Jeni Wittrock.
pages cm.—(Pebble plus. Pets Up Close)
Summary: "Full-color, zoomed-in photos and simple text describe pet rabbits' body parts"—Provided by publisher.
Audience: Ages 5-8.
Audience: K to grade 3.
Includes bibliographical references and index.
ISBN 978-1-4914-0584-0 (library binding)
ISBN 978-1-4914-0618-2 (ebook pdf)
1. Rabbits—Juvenile literature. I. Title.
SF453.2.W58 2015
636.932—dc23                                        2014012288

**Editorial Credits**
Bobbie Nuytten, designer; Svetlana Zhurkin, media researcher; Katy LaVigne, production specialist; Sarah Schuette, photo stylist; Marcy Morin, photo scheduler

**Photo Credits**
Capstone Studio: Karon Dubke, 9, 15, 17, 21; Shutterstock: Andrey Medvedev, cover (front), Atitude, cover (background), bogdanhoda, 1, Dagmar Hijmans, 5, indigolotos, 7, Loskutnikov, 11, Marina Jay, 13, Polaric, 19

The author dedicates this book to her beloved companion rabbits, Baxter, Dallas, and Opal; they are always in her heart. Binky free, sweet ones.

## Note to Parents and Teachers

The Pets Up Close set supports national science standards related to life science. This book describes and illustrates pet rabbits. The images support early readers in understanding the text. The repetition of words and phrases helps early readers learn new words. This book also introduces early readers to subject-specific vocabulary words, which are defined in the Glossary section. Early readers may need assistance to read some words and to use the Table of Contents, Glossary, Read More, Internet Sites, and Index sections of the book.

Printed in the United States of America in North Mankato, Minnesota
052014      008087CGF14

# Table of Contents

# Alert! Alert!

What was that?

Rabbits have perfect body parts to stay safe and alert. Let's take an up-close look at these cute and curious pets.

# Rabbit Ears

Rabbits' ears can be big or
small, short or tall, up or down.
Rabbits' ears turn all around.
They can listen for trouble
in any direction.

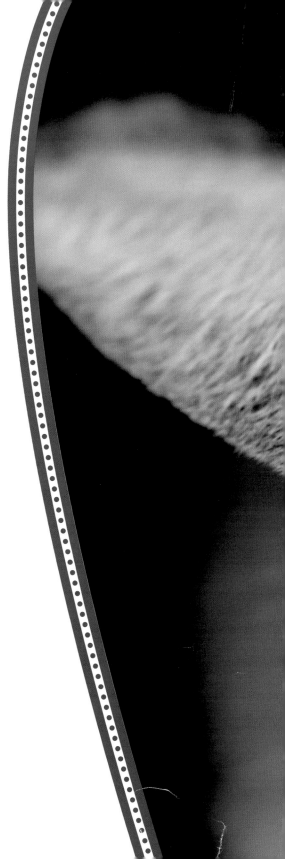

7

# Rabbit Eyes

Rabbits' big eyes are on the sides of their heads. They can even see what's behind them. Good eyesight helps rabbits spot danger.

9

# Rabbit Noses

Sniff, sniff!

Rabbits' wiggling noses smell everything around them. Rabbits often smell or hear predators before they see them.

11

# Rabbit Teeth

It's easy to see a rabbit's big front teeth. The other teeth are far back in their mouths. Strong teeth help rabbits chew tough food like twigs and hay.

# Rabbit Whiskers

Will I fit? Rabbit whiskers feel

everything around them, even

in the dark. Whiskers sense

if a rabbit can fit through

a small space.

# Rabbit Feet

If there's trouble, rabbits thump a warning with their big back feet. Thick fur keeps bunny toes warm and protected.

# Rabbit Fur

Rabbits' fur can be long or short.

Warm fur protects bunnies' skin from sun, wind, and rain.

No matter the weather, always house your pet rabbit indoors.

# Rabbit Tails

Short, round, and fluffy, bunnies' tails never get in their way. From end to end, rabbits are amazing pets!

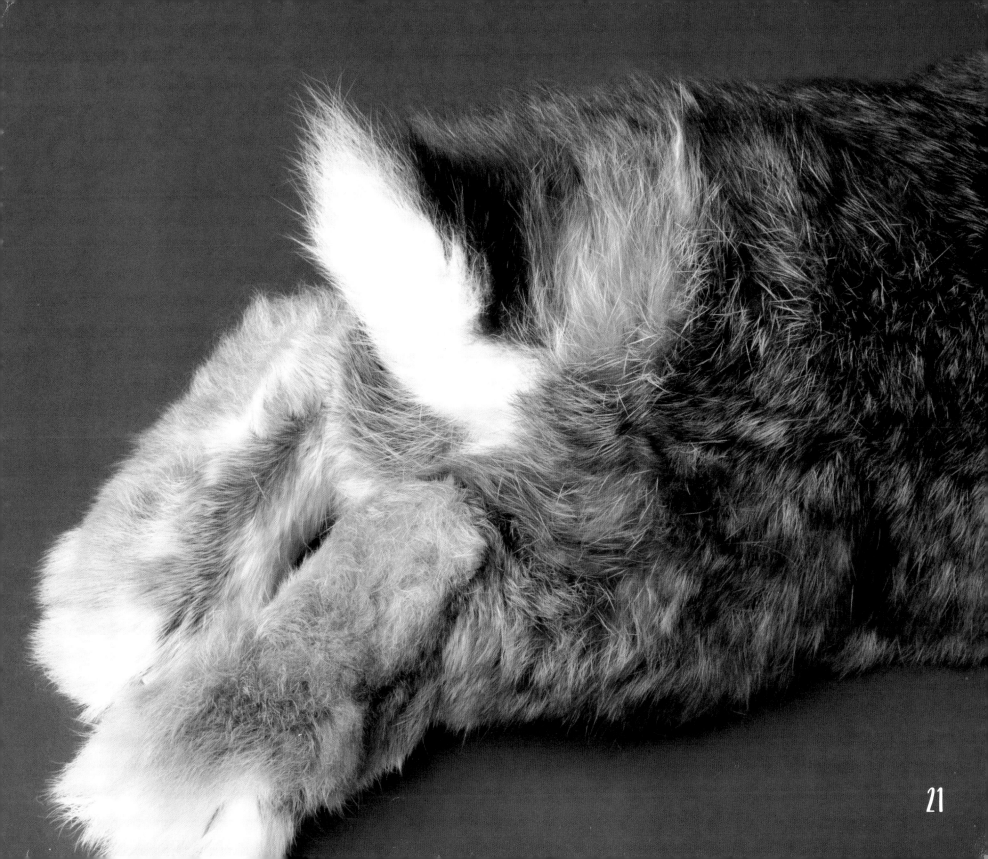

# Glossary

**alert**—awake and paying attention

**curious**—eager to explore and learn about new things

**danger**—a situation that is not safe

**predator**—an animal that hunts other animals for food

**protect**—to keep safe

**sense**—to feel

**thump**—to pound the ground with both back feet; rabbits thump to warn of danger

**twig**—a small stick or branch; some twigs are safe for bunnies to eat

**wiggle**—to quickly move up and down

# Read More

**Ganeri, Anita**. *Bunny's Guide to Caring for Your Rabbit.* Pets' Guides. Chicago: Heinemann, 2013.

**Heos, Bridget**. *Do You Really Want a Rabbit?* Do You Really Want...? Mankato, Minn.: Amicus, 2014.

**Olson, Gillia**. *Cats Up Close.* Pets Up Close. Mankato, Minn.: Capstone Press, 2014.

# Internet Sites

FactHound offers a safe, fun way to find Internet sites related to this book. All of the sites on FactHound have been researched by our staff.

Here's all you do:

Visit *www.facthound.com*

Type in this code: 9781491405840

Check out projects, games and lots more at
**www.capstonekids.com**

23

SHOREWOOD-TROY LIBRARY

# Index

Word Count: 211
Grade: 1
Early-Intervention Level: 16